BIG PICTURE  SPORTS

Meet the
TAMPA BAY
BUCCANEERS

BY
ZACK BURGESS

NORWOODHOUSE PRESS

CHICAGO, ILLINOIS

NORWOODHOUSE PRESS

P.O. Box 316598 • Chicago, Illinois 60631
For more information about Norwood House Press please visit our website at
www.norwoodhousepress.com or call 866-565-2900.

Photo Credits:
All photos courtesy of Associated Press, except for the following: Fleer Corp. (6, 11 middle & bottom),
Black Book Archives (7, 8, 15, 16, 18, 23), Topps, Inc. (10 both, 11 top).

Cover Photo: Al Messerschmidt/Associated Press

The football memorabilia photographed for this book is part of the authors' collection. The collectibles used
for artistic background purposes in this series were manufactured by many different card companies—
including Bowman, Donruss, Fleer, Leaf, O-Pee-Chee, Pacific, Panini America, Philadelphia Chewing Gum,
Pinnacle, Pro Line, Pro Set, Score, Topps, and Upper Deck—as well as several food brands, including
Crane's, Hostess, Kellogg's, McDonald's and Post.

Designer: Ron Jaffe
Series Editors: Mike Kennedy and Mark Stewart
Project Management: Black Book Partners, LLC.
Editorial Production: Lisa Walsh

LIBRARY OF CONGRESS CATALOGING-IN-PUBLICATION DATA
    Names: Burgess, Zack.
    Title: Meet the Tampa Bay Buccaneers / by Zack Burgess.
    Description: Chicago, Illinois : Norwood House Press, [2016] | Series: Big
        picture sports | Includes bibliographical references and index. |
        Audience: Grade: K to Grade 3.
    Identifiers: LCCN 2015024577| ISBN 9781599537276 (Library Edition : alk.
        paper) | ISBN 9781603578301 (eBook)
    Subjects: LCSH: Tampa Bay Buccaneers (Football team)--Miscellanea--Juvenile
        literature.
    Classification: LCC GV956.T35 B87 2016 | DDC 796.332/640975965--dc23
    LC record available at http://lccn.loc.gov/2015024577

288N—072016
Manufactured in the United States of America in North Mankato, Minnesota

CONTENTS

Words in **bold type** are defined on page 24.

The Buccaneers celebrate a score.

4

CALL ME A BUCCANEER

A "buccaneer" is another name for a pirate. The Tampa Bay Buccaneers attack with the speed and daring of adventurers on the high seas. They always play to win. The "Bucs" are on a quest for football's greatest treasure, a Super Bowl championship.

TIME MACHINE

The Buccaneers played their first season in the National Football League (NFL) in 1976. They lost their first 26 games. Since then, the Buccaneers have been at their best with a strong defense. Two of their biggest stars were safety **John Lynch** and linebacker Derrick Brooks.

JOHN LYNCH — Safety

Derrick Brooks keeps his eyes on the ball.

The pirate ship is a favorite of Buccaneers fans.

BEST SEAT IN THE HOUSE

The Buccaneers play their home games in a warm and sunny stadium. It is on the west coast of Florida. At one end of the field is a huge pirate ship. Its cannons fire whenever the team scores. The ship looks real. But it would not float in water.

RUNNING BACK

RICKY BUCCA

SHOE BOX

The trading cards on these pages show some of the best Buccaneers ever.

LEE ROY SELMON

DEFENSIVE END · 1976–1984
Lee Roy and his brother, Dewey, starred for the Buccaneers. Lee Roy was named **All-Pro** in 1979.

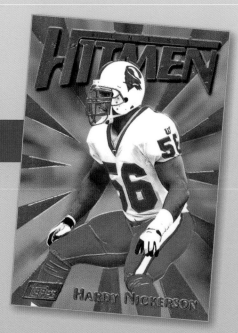

HARDY NICKERSON

LINEBACKER · 1993–1999
Hardy was one of the NFL's top linebackers of the 1990s. He was the team's hardest tackler.

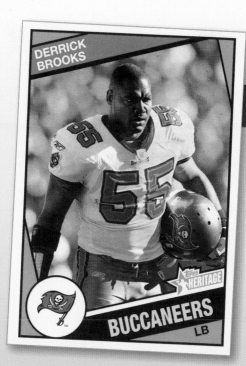

DERRICK BROOKS

LINEBACKER · 1995-2008

Many fans believe Derrick was the best player in team history. He was the NFL Defensive Player of the Year in 2002.

MIKE ALSTOTT

FULLBACK · 1996-2006

Mike was a rugged running back. Fans loved him for his team spirit.

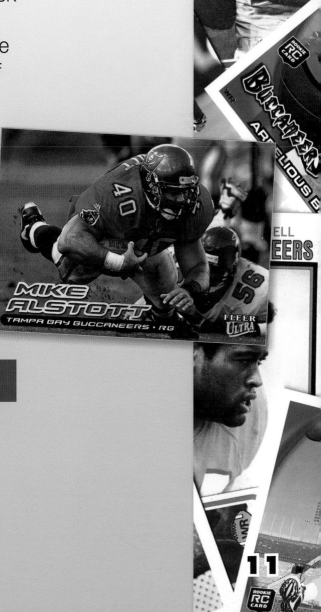

SIMEON RICE

DEFENSIVE END · 2001-2006

Simeon loved to tackle opposing quarterbacks. His nickname was the "Sackmaster."

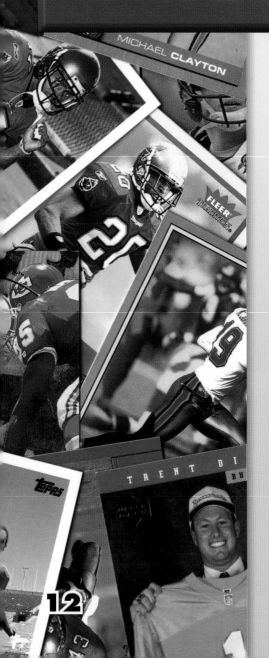

THE BIG PICTURE

Look at the two photos on page 13. Both appear to be the same. But they are not. There are three differences. Can you spot them?

Answers on page 23.

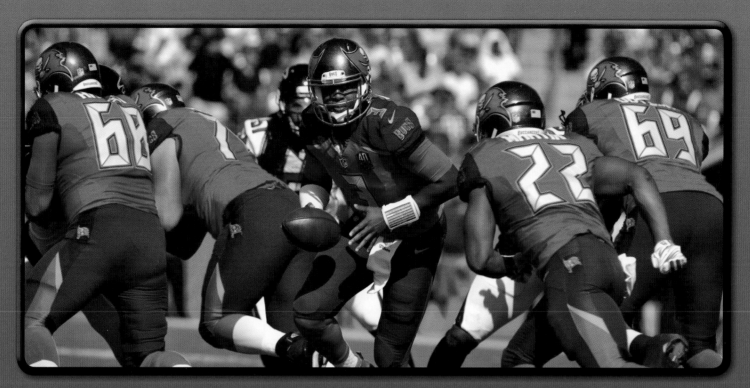

13

TRUE OR FALSE?

Ronde Barber was a star defender. Two of these facts about him are **TRUE**. One is **FALSE**. Do you know which is which?

1 Ronde holds the team record for **interceptions** with 47.

2 Ronde liked to wear a pirate's eyepatch during games.

3 Ronde's twin brother, Tiki, was also an NFL star.

Answer on page 23.

Ronde Barber returns an interception.

Buccaneers fans love to dress up for games.

Go Buccaneers, Go!

There is no party like a pirate party. Buccaneers fans make sure of this. Every game is a chance for them to dress up with face paint and costumes. Some look funny. Others look scary. The Buccaneers can always count on their fans to make lots of noise.

y Selmon

ON THE MAP

Here is a look at where five Buccaneers were born, along with a fun fact about each.

 KEYSHAWN JOHNSON • LOS ANGELES, CALIFORNIA
Keyshawn caught 106 passes for the Buccaneers in 2001.

 JOHN LYNCH • HINSDALE, ILLINOIS
John made the **Pro Bowl** five times for the Buccaneers.

 JAMES WILDER • SIKESTON, MISSOURI
James ran for 1,544 yards and 13 touchdowns in 1984.

 DOUG WILLIAMS • ZACHARY, LOUISIANA
Doug led the Buccaneers to the **playoffs** for the first time in 1979.

 MARTIN GRAMATICA • BUENOS AIRES, ARGENTINA
Martin was the first player from his country to score points in a Super Bowl.

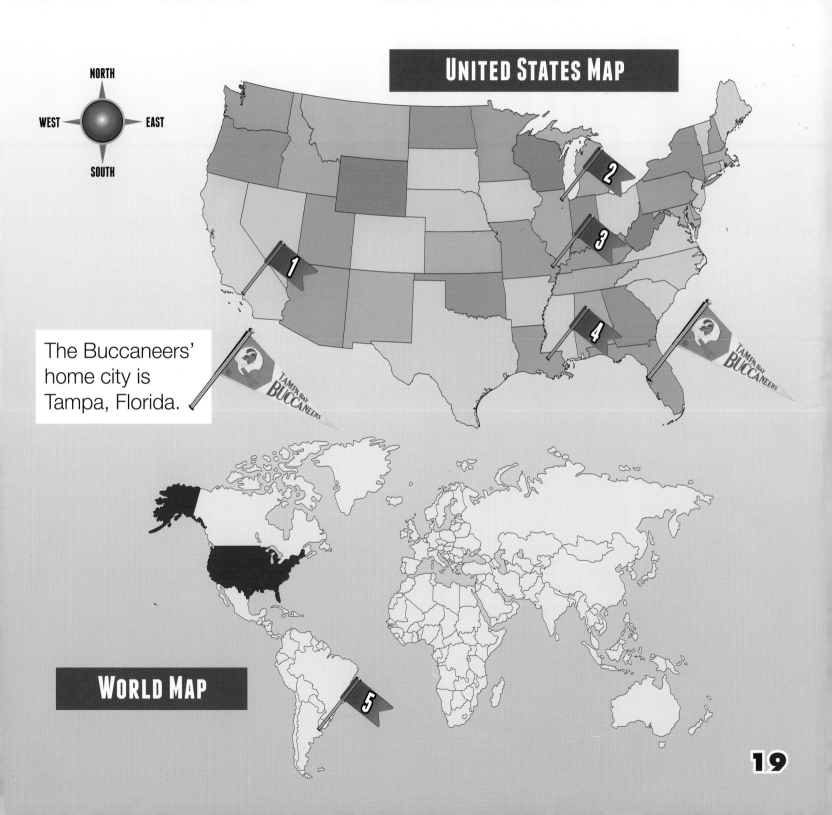

NORTH

WEST ● EAST

SOUTH

The Buccaneers' home city is Tampa, Florida.

WORLD MAP

Home and Away

Mike Evans wears the Buccaneers' home uniform.

Football teams wear different uniforms for home and away games. For many years, the Buccaneers wore orange, white, and red. In the 1990s, they changed to red and a silver-brown color called pewter.

Jameis Winston wears the Buccaneers' away uniform.

The Buccaneers' helmet is pewter with a red flag on each side. On that flag is a skull and crossed swords. For a long time, the team used a picture of a pirate on its helmet.

WE WON!

The Buccaneers reached the Super Bowl for the first time at the end of the 2002 season. Many fans thought they would lose. Coach Jon Gruden and the Buccaneers proved them wrong. **Dexter Jackson** led a great defensive effort. Tampa Bay won 48–21.

RECORD BOOK

These Buccaneers set team records.

PASSING YARDS	RECORD
Season: **Josh Freeman** (2012)	4,065
Career: Vinny Testaverde	14,820

TOUCHDOWN CATCHES	RECORD
Season: Mike Evans (2014)	12
Career: Jimmie Giles	34

RUSHING YARDS	RECORD
Season: James Wilder (1984)	1,544
Career: James Wilder	5,957

ANSWERS FOR THE BIG PICTURE
#22 changed to #52, the logo on #68's helmet disappeared, and the football changed to a basketball.

ANSWER FOR TRUE AND FALSE
#2 is false. Ronde never wore a pirate's eyepatch during games.

FOOTBALL WORDS

INDEX

All-Pro
An honor given to the best NFL player at each position.

Interceptions
Passes caught by a defensive player.

Playoffs
The games played after the regular season that decide which teams will play in the Super Bowl.

Pro Bowl
The NFL's annual all-star game.

Photos are on **BOLD** numbered pages.

ABOUT THE AUTHOR

Zack Burgess has been writing about sports for more than 20 years. He has lived all over the country and interviewed lots of All-Pro football players, including Brett Favre, Eddie George, Jerome Bettis, Shannon Sharpe, and Rich Gannon. Zack was the first African American beat writer to cover Major League Baseball when he worked for the *Kansas City Star*.

ABOUT THE BUCCANEERS

Learn more at these websites:
www.buccaneers.com • www.profootballhof.com
www.teamspiritextras.com/Overtime/html/buccaneers.html